Native American

Your Cookbook of Traditional, Healthy Dish Ideas!

BY: Allie Allen

COOK & ENJOY

Copyright 2020 Allie Allen

Copyright Notes

This book is written as an informational tool. While the author has taken every precaution to ensure the accuracy of the information provided therein, the reader is warned that they assume all risk when following the content. The author will not be held responsible for any damages that may occur as a result of the readers' actions.

The author does not give permission to reproduce this book in any form, including but not limited to: print, social media posts, electronic copies or photocopies, unless permission is expressly given in writing.

Table of Contents

Introduction 6

1 – Choctaw Stew 8

2 – Venison Stew 10

3 – Jicama Salad 13

4 – Poyha Meat & Corn Meal 15

5 – Prickly Pear & Bean Casserole 18

6 – Three Sisters Soup 20

7 – Corn & Onion Soup 22

8 – Salmon Cakes 24

9 – Egg & Zucchini Salad 26

10 – Black Bean Soup 28

11 – Choctaw Wild Onions 30

12 – Wild Turkey Roast 32

13 – Acorn Bread 34

14 – Spicy Turkey with Chilies 36

15 – Baked New Potatoes 38

16 – Pemmican 40

17 – Choctaw Bread Banaha 42

18 – Pine Nut & Cumin Catfish 44

19 – Osage Meat Soup 46

20 – Fried Green Tomatoes 48

21 – Sweet Potato Salsa 50

22 – Native American Succotash 53

23 – Butternut Squash & Bell Pepper Soup 55

24 – Native Frybread 57

25 – Vegetable Sauté 59

26 – Gitigan Salad 61

27 – Dakota Wojapi Berry Sauce 64

28 – Wild Rice Burgers 66

29 – Peach & Blueberry Salsa 68

30 – Cherokee Fried Hominy 70

There are many desserts that were first made by Native Americans. Here are some of the best…

.... 72

31 – Corn Meal Cookies 73

32 – Grilled Pineapple 76

33 – Cherokee Grape Dumplings 78

34 – Dessert Fruit Salad 81

35 – Choctaw Autumn Cake 83

Conclusion 86

About the Author 87

Author's Afterthoughts 89

Introduction

Are you interested in bringing Native American dishes to life?

Can you find the typical ingredients or suitable substitutes to make the recipes authentic?

Do you know what types of foods were used most often by Native Americans?

The original "Americans" used many ingredients in their dishes, but none were more common than squash, corns and beans. These were the staple foods on which their menu was focused. They ate corn from the cob and also ground it into cornmeal for other recipes. Various beans were used, especially in the Southwest. Squash is used almost as often now as it was in traditional recipes.

Before settlers from Europe arrived in North America, native peoples had become skilled farmers. In addition to natural ingredients, they used many herbs, vegetables and wild grains in their dishes. Some include pumpkins, mint, sage, onions, cabbage, mushrooms, nuts and other ingredients.

Native Americans used venison in many meat dishes. They also used pork, mutton, buffalo and rabbit, in addition to freshwater and saltwater fish and shellfish.

Try these Native American recipes out in your home and wow your family and guests…

1 – Choctaw Stew

This is a simple recipe indigenous to Native Americans. It tastes the best during the summer months when the gardens are producing plenty of vegetables.

Makes 2-4 Servings

Cooking + Prep Time: 10 minutes + 6 hours slow cooker time

Ingredients:

- 3 peeled potatoes, white
- 6 peeled carrots, large
- 1 chopped onion, large, white
- Corn from 5 cobs, fresh
- 3 cups of beans, green
- 1 cup of peas, sweet
- 5 cups of broth, your favorite type
- Salt, kosher, as desired
- Pepper, ground, as desired

Optional: Garlic; jalapenos; yellow squash, chopped; roasted green, chopped chilies, as desired

Instructions:

1. Prepare vegetables by peeling and chopping, as needed.

2. Add ingredients including broth to large-sized slow cooker. Allow it to cook for six hours or longer on the High setting. Serve.

2 – Venison Stew

This is a popular Native American recipe. The stew is hearty and works well to warm you up on cold days. If you prefer, you can use goat, Buffalo or beef instead of venison.

Makes 6 Servings

Cooking + Prep Time: 40 minutes

Ingredients:

- 1 & 1/2 lbs. of cubed venison
- 1/4 cup of oil, corn
- 1 chopped onion, medium
- 5 chopped onions, green
- 3 diced garlic cloves, large
- 8 quartered small potatoes, red
- 1 cubed rutabaga, small
- 3 diced stalks of celery
- 1 cubed pepper, red
- 2 bay leaves, fresh
- 1 cup of cubed mushrooms, wild
- 1/4 tsp. of chopped parsley, dried
- 1/4 tsp. of salt, coarse
- Pepper, ground, as desired
- 1 tbsp. of vinegar, apple cider
- 2 cups of beef or vegetable broth or filtered water
- 2 cans of tomatoes, stewed
- A pinch sassafras powder

Instructions:

1. In large pot, heat the oil on med-high. Add the venison. Brown each side.

2. Add garlic and onions and cook for two more minutes. Add the remainder of ingredients, except for sassafras. Blend and stir well.

3. Cover pot. Cook for 1/2 hour, till venison, potatoes and rutabaga become tender.

4. Remove stew from the heat. Add pinch sassafras powder. Stir well again.

5. If you prefer a spicier stew, add three or four red chili peppers or jalapeno peppers and add one tsp. of hot sauce as you are cooking. Serve.

3 – Jicama Salad

Jicama is starchy, crunchy tubers originally grown in Mexico. They are used as salad ingredients, as well as a type of appetizer served with dip.

Makes 1-2 Servings

Cooking + Prep Time: 10 minutes + 1 hour refrigeration time

Ingredients:

- 1 peeled jicama, cubed
- 2 to 4 roasted & peeled chilies, large
- 2 fresh limes, juice only
- Salt, kosher & pepper, ground, as desired

Instructions:

1. Use a potato peeler to peel jicama. Cut it into small-sized cubes. Pour into medium bowl.

2. Add the chilies. Squeeze limes' juice into bowl. Combine well.

3. Cover the bowl. Place in refrigerator for an hour, then serve.

4 – Poyha Meat & Corn Meal

This recipe that uses venison was handed down through generations of Cherokee. It is best described as meatloaf or cornbread with meat added.

Makes 8-10 Servings

Cooking + Prep Time: 1 hour & 10 minutes

Ingredients:

- 2 pounds of ground chicken or ground turkey
- 3 tbsp. of oil, vegetable
- 3 chopped bacon slices
- 2 x 14-oz. cans of drained corn, whole kernel – may substitute 2 cups of frozen, thawed whole kernel corn
- 2 cups of finely chopped green grapes, seedless
- 1 diced large onion, yellow
- 3 eggs, large
- 1 & 1/4 cups of coarse corn meal, yellow
- 1/2 tsp. of pepper, ground
- Non-stick spray

Optional: paprika, sweet

Optional: 1/2 tsp. of salt, garlic

Instructions:

1. In food processor, chop corn till it is in very small-sized pieces. Don't allow it to liquify. Set the corn aside.

2. In a large bowl, add the chopped corn, along with grapes, eggs, onions and ground pepper. Beat till eggs have mixed well. Set them aside. This is the point where you'll add the optional garlic salt or paprika, if you desire.

3. Cook the ground meat in oil till barely browned. Be sure you don't overcook it. Add the drained meat to the corn mixture. Wipe out the skillet using paper towels. Season with a bit of oil.

4. Add corn meal to the corn and meat mixture. Combine well, using your hands. Add additional corn meal, a bit at a time. You want a moist texture, not a runny one. Transfer to Dutch oven and cover it.

5. Place Dutch oven on your outdoor grill on med. heat for 50 minutes to an hour. Cool for 15 minutes or longer. Slice meat in Dutch oven. Lift the slices from Dutch oven and transfer to a large dish. Serve.

5 – Prickly Pear & Bean Casserole

Prickly pears adapt well to growing in the desert. They are rich in fiber and a healthy addition to any dish. This recipe includes wild oregano and sumac berries as well, but you can use cinnamon instead if you can't find those at local farmer's markets.

Makes 10-12+ Servings

Cooking + Prep Time: 1 hour & 15 minutes

Ingredients:

- 2 pounds of cleaned and soaked tepary beans, white – you can substitute navy or pinto beans
- 1 pound of prickly pear tender pads, spines removed, diced – you can substitute kiwi fruit
- 4 green onions with minced shoots
- 4 minced garlic cloves
- 4 tsp. sumac berries, ground – you can substitute cinnamon
- 4 tsp. of oregano leaves, wild, dried and crushed – you can substitute cinnamon
- 6 tsp. of oil, olive
- 2 tsp. salt, kosher

Instructions:

1. Boil beans till they are very tender. Remove from the heat. Drain them well.

2. In wok or skillet, heat 1 tsp. oil. Toss in prickle pear pad pieces. Sauté for three to five minutes. Add wild oregano, onions and garlic. Continue heating over low heat for three more minutes.

3. Pour beans into baking dish with extra space than that needed just for beans. Add and stir in prickly pear pads, garlic, onion and the spices.

4. Preheat the oven to 300F.

5. Pour remainder of oil into beans. Sprinkle with sumac berries. Cover. Bake for 30 minutes and serve while hot.

6 – Three Sisters Soup

This soup is named after three crops planted together traditionally by Native American people. The crops are winter squash, corn and beans. This recipe includes all three.

Makes 4 Servings

Cooking + Prep Time: 1 hour & 55 minutes

Ingredients:

- 4 pounds of squash, winter
- 2 small, diced onions, yellow
- 1/4 cup of oil, olive
- 2 tsp. of thyme, dried
- 1/4 cup of chopped garlic
- 1 tsp. of pepper, ground
- 4 quarts of stock, vegetable
- 1/2 cup of wine, white
- 1 bay leaf, large
- 4 cans of beans, cannellini
- 1 pound of whole kernel corn
- 1 bunch of sliced onions, green

Instructions:

1. Preheat the oven to 350F. Halve the squash, then remove the seeds. Roast for about 40 minutes. Let the squash cool. Remove flesh & save liquid in squash. Blend the squash in the food processor till smooth.

2. In large-sized pot, sauté the onions in oil on med. heat till brown. Add garlic, thyme & ground pepper. Stir till garlic has turned brown.

3. Add stock slowly. Add squash, wine and bay leaf. Allow the mixture to simmer for several minutes, and then add green onions, beans and corn. Simmer for 18-20 minutes and serve.

7 – Corn & Onion Soup

There are several ways that corn soup is made. This recipe uses a method that does not include milk or cream, which some other recipes call for.

Makes 3-4 Servings

Cooking + Prep Time: 25 minutes

Ingredients:

- 3 cups of stock, turkey or vegetable
- 4 cups of corn, sweet
- 1 large red or orange bell pepper, chopped
- 1 chopped onion, white
- 2 tbsp. of oil, vegetable
- Salt, kosher & pepper, ground, as desired
- Garlic, as desired

Instructions:

1. Heat 2 tbsp. oil in a frying pan on med. heat. When it is hot, add the onions, corn and peppers. Sauté for six to eight minutes, till tender.

2. Add vegetable mixture to a food processor. Mix with stock till you achieve the consistency you prefer. A chunkier texture is tasty. Serve.

8 – Salmon Cakes

This recipe was passed through the generations by Native Americans. The cakes are easily cooked and a delicious appetizer for any lunch or dinner.

Makes 2-4 Servings

Cooking + Prep Time: 1 hour & 5 minutes

Ingredients:

- 1 pound can of flaked salmon, liquid reserved
- 1/2 cup of cornmeal
- 4 berries, Juniper
- 1/3 cup of milk, whole
- 2 lightly beaten eggs, large

Instructions:

1. Mix salmon, cornmeal and Juniper berries together. Carefully add eggs.

2. Slowly & carefully add milk. Be sure you don't have too much liquid. You are just moistening ingredients. Some salmon liquid can also be carefully added.

3. After batter is moist enough to pack, made small cakes, 2" wide and 1" high, for appetizers.

4. Grease a baking pan. Place cakes on it. Bake in 350F oven for 1/2 hour. Serve hot or cold. You can serve them with tarter sauce or mayo, if you like.

9 – Egg & Zucchini Salad

You can use this recipe as a hearty side dish or an entrée if you add meat. This is a popular dish to take to carry-in dinners.

Makes 8-10 Servings

Cooking + Prep Time: 15 minutes

Ingredients:

- 5 cups greens, like spinach, mint or dandelion
- 1 cup of tomatoes, cherry
- 1 cup of beans, green
- 1 cup of corn, sweet
- 1 cup of chopped zucchini, raw
- 1 cup of peas, sweet
- 1 cup of carrots, shredded
- 1 cup of mushrooms, sliced
- 1/2 cup of mozzarella cheese shreds
- 1/4 cup of pecans or pine nuts
- 3 hard-boiled eggs, large, sliced
- 1 or 2 sliced avocados
- 1/2 cup of beets, pickled
- 1/4 cup of olives, black

Instructions:

1. Add all the ingredients to large-sized bowl. You can add or delete any ingredients, to make the salad to your liking.

2. Add light salad dressing if you like, or serve "dry".

10 – Black Bean Soup

Black bean soup is a great winter dish. It keeps you warm and full. This delicious soup will be a great choice for a snowy evening dinner.

Makes 10-12 Servings

Cooking + Prep Time: 1 hour & 5 minutes

Ingredients:

- 2 pounds of beans, black
- 1 cup of sliced leeks
- 1/8 cup of pepper, ground
- 1/2 cup of water, filtered
- 2 garlic cloves
- 1/3 cup of oil, vegetable

Instructions:

1. In large pan, sauté leeks till they are golden and crispy. Add the garlic and 1/2 of beans. Smash beans for a thicker consistency.

2. Add remainder of beans, but don't mash them.

3. Add water, kosher salt and ground pepper. Simmer for 35-40 minutes and serve.

11 – Choctaw Wild Onions

Wild onions can be used in many types of dishes. You can serve them with squash, scrambled eggs or atop baked potatoes.

Makes 2-3 Servings

Cooking + Prep Time: 15 minutes

Ingredients:

- 1 cup wild onions, chopped, peeled outer bulb potion, with roots cut away – you can substitute spring onions if you like
- 1 cup stock, vegetable
- 1/2 tsp. of pepper, ground
- 1/2 tsp. of garlic

Instructions:

1. Heat a skillet or frying pan. Add stock and onions. Cook onions till water is nearly gone. Add seasonings as desired.

2. Serve as a simple side or add to other recipes.

12 – Wild Turkey Roast

If you love family gatherings with delicious food, then roasted turkey is a great choice. It will serve your entire family and add a wonderful taste to your dinner.

Makes 8-10 Servings

Cooking + Prep Time: 3 hours & 25 minutes

Ingredients:

- 1 turkey, 8-10 lbs., wild if available
- 1 onion, medium
- 2 apples, medium
- 1 tsp. of sage
- 2 celery stalks
- 6 to 8 bacon slices
- Bacon fat, melted
- Salt, kosher & pepper, ground, as desired

Instructions:

1. Preheat oven to 325F.

2. Sprinkle outside and inside of turkey with kosher salt & ground pepper. Cut onions and apples in halves. Slice stalks of celery. Place apples, onions, sage and celery inside cavity.

3. Sprinkle turkey with more kosher salt & ground pepper. Cover breast with slices of bacon and a cheesecloth that has been soaked in the bacon fat.

4. Roast in 325F oven till joints are freely moving, 3 hours or so. Baste turkey frequently with juices from pan. Serve.

13 – Acorn Bread

When you think about Native American dishes made from grain, remember acorn bread. This is a wonderful bread that everyone likes.

Makes Various # of Servings

Cooking + Prep Time: 1 hour & 25 minutes + sitting time

Ingredients:

- 2 cups of finely ground meal, acorn
- 6 tbsp. of cornmeal
- 2 cups of flour, all-purpose
- 1 packet of dry yeast, active
- 1/2 cup of water, cold
- 1 cup of water, boiling
- 1/4 cup of water, lukewarm
- 1 tsp. of salt, kosher
- 1 tbsp. of butter, softened
- 1 cup of potatoes, mashed

Instructions:

1. In large bowl, add cold water and corn meal. Blend together while adding boiling water. Cook for several minutes. Add butter and salt. Mix well and let it sit till it's lukewarm.

2. In separate bowl, add lukewarm water and allow it to soften dry yeast mixed with it. After it is done, add to ingredients from step 1.

3. Knead mixture thoroughly, till it forms a sticky dough. Let it sit till dough has doubled in size. Make loaves from dough. Allow to rise again.

4. Place loaves in 375F oven. Bake for 40-45 minutes. Serve.

14 – Spicy Turkey with Chilies

This is an excellent meal, especially when served in the summer months. The spice and heat of the prepared turkey go nicely with cool guacamole and salad.

Makes 2-3 Servings

Cooking + Prep Time: 20 minutes + 4 to 5 slow cooker hours

Ingredients:

- 1 turkey breast, large, boneless
- 2 chopped onions, white
- 2 crushed garlic cloves
- 1 & 1/2 cups of salsa, hot
- 4 jalapenos, sliced
- 1 to 2 cups of green chilies, roasted, peeled
- 1 tbsp. of pepper, ground

Instructions:

1. Add ingredients to a slow cooker. Cook for four to five hours on the Medium setting.

2. When cooked through, shred the turkey meat.

3. Use guacamole to garnish, as desired. Serve.

15 – Baked New Potatoes

These potatoes are often served with burgers and similar foods, instead of serving French fries. They're a tasty side for other meals, too.

Makes 6-8 Servings

Cooking + Prep Time: 35 minutes

Ingredients:

- 10 potatoes, new, red
- 3 tbsp. of oil, olive
- Spices, optional, as desired:
- Salt, kosher
- Pepper, ground
- 1/2 tsp. of garlic
- 1/2 tsp. of oregano
- 4 tsp. of rosemary, ground

Instructions:

1. Preheat the oven to 350F.

2. Scrub the potatoes. Cut in fourths. Leave skins on.

3. Place the potatoes in large sized plastic bag. Add 2-3 tbsp. oil. Add amounts you desire of salt, pepper, oregano, garlic and rosemary. Don't over-salt.

4. Transfer potatoes to oiled baking sheet. Bake in 350F oven for 20 minutes, or till done. Serve while hot.

16 – Pemmican

Pemmican will give you instant energy, especially if you're on a long trip. It is nutritious and filling and has been eaten by Native Americans for hundreds of years.

Makes Various # of Servings

Cooking + Prep Time: 25 minutes + 8 hours refrigeration time

Ingredients:

- 1 cup of chopped nuts, roasted
- 1 cup of raisins, dark or golden
- 4 tbsp. of peanuts, shelled
- 3 cups of butter, softened
- 2 tbsp. of honey, pure
- 1/3 tsp. of chili powder
- 1 cup of Jerky, ground

Instructions:

1. Mix all ingredients together. Press into shallow pan. Cover pan with waxed paper. Place in refrigerator overnight.

2. Cut into circle shapes or bars. Serve. Wrap extras in foil. They will last for a good while as long as you're not in a very hot area.

17 – Choctaw Bread Banaha

Corn and recipes that use corn are favorites among many Native Americans. Banaha is somewhat like a tamale, except it typically has no filling. It is often served topped with salsa.

Makes 2-4 Servings

Cooking + Prep Time: 1 hour & 20 minutes

Ingredients:

- 2 cups corn meal
- 1 & 1/2 cups of water, boiling
- 5 to 7 shucks of corn
- Salt, kosher, as desired

Instructions:

1. Boil the corn shucks about 10-12 minutes.

2. In large-sized bowl, mix water, corn meal and kosher salt together till it has a doughy consistency.

3. Roll into long shapes that will easily fit inside corn shucks.

4. Wrap shucks around dough pieces. Tie shut with shuck string. Add to boiling water in a pot on medium heat and cook for 30 to 40 minutes. Then drain well.

5. Allow banaha to sit for about five minutes, then serve. Top with salsa, if you like.

18 – Pine Nut & Cumin Catfish

Native American recipes must include a favorite fish. This recipe for catfish is delicious, and it also offers protein in your diet.

Makes 4 Servings

Cooking + Prep Time: 35 minutes

Ingredients:

- 4 fillets, catfish
- 1/4 cup of oil, vegetable
- 1/4 cup + 2 tbsp. of pine nuts, toasted
- 1/2 cup of cornmeal, yellow
- 1/4 cup of flour, all-purpose
- 1/2 tsp. of pepper, cayenne
- 1 tsp. of salt, kosher
- 1/4 tsp. of cumin, ground

Instructions:

1. Preheat the oven to 350F.

2. Spread pine nuts on cookie sheet. Place in 350F oven for five minutes, till toasted. Separate 2 tbsp. for later.

3. Grind 1/4 cup pine nuts. Add to bowl with fillets. Add cornmeal, cayenne pepper, kosher salt, cumin and flour. Coat fillets thoroughly.

4. Heat the oil in large-sized skillet on medium heat. Fry coated fillets till both sides are golden brown in color. Sprinkle on extra pine nuts and serve.

19 – Osage Meat Soup

This is an indigenous, traditional recipe of Native Americans. It has been preserved by tribal historians and uses buffalo meat as a prime source of protein.

Makes 12 Servings

Cooking + Prep Time: 1 hour & 35 minutes

Ingredients:

- 3-4 lbs. buffalo meat
- Salt, kosher, if desired

Instructions:

1. Cut the buffalo meat in strips, following grain, about 1 & 1/2 – 2" long and as thick as your thumb. Wash well.

2. Add meat to pot with cold, filtered water covering meat by only an inch. Mash meat with a ladle.

3. Leave pot uncovered and boil for 50 minutes to one hour. Serve hot.

20 – Fried Green Tomatoes

Yes, Native Americans originated fried green tomatoes before the settlers even came to what would be the United States. It has subtle differences, but it's the original recipe.

Makes 4-6 Servings

Cooking + Prep Time: 40 minutes

Ingredients:

- 3 or 4 large tomatoes, green
- 2 cups of ground cornmeal, yellow
- 1 tbsp. of salt, kosher
- A pinch of pepper, ground

For frying: oil, vegetable

Instructions:

1. Slice tomatoes in pieces. Sprinkle salt over them. Allow to set for 10 minutes or so. Pat dry with paper towels.

2. Add cornmeal to medium bowl. Dip tomato slices in it. They should be covered in cornmeal on each side.

3. Heat a little oil in medium pan. Fry tomatoes till golden brown in color. Serve with sour cream and coriander leaves, if you desire.

21 – Sweet Potato Salsa

This salsa is filled with flavors from the sweet potatoes, so it's refreshing yet hearty. You can serve it with chips or other dipping ingredients.

Makes Various # of Servings

Cooking + Prep Time: 50 minutes

Ingredients:

- 4 sweet potatoes, medium
- 1 large onion, sweet
- 3 jalapenos, raw – remove seeds before using
- 1 chopped bell pepper, red
- Olive oil, to drizzle

Optional: 1 or 2 tomatoes, large

- 1 fresh lime, juice only
- Chili powder, as desired
- Cumin, as desired
- Salt, kosher, as desired
- Pepper, black, as desired
- Garlic, as desired

Instructions:

1. Preheat the oven to 350F.

2. Peel sweet potatoes. Dice them finely.

3. Pour potatoes and desired spices into large bowl. Drizzle oil over top. Mix well.

4. Spread the sweet potatoes on a baking sheet. Bake in 350F oven for 18-20 minutes, till tender.

5. Place chopped tomatoes, sautéed pepper and jalapenos in your food processor. Chop finely.

6. Mix all ingredients in a large-sized bowl. Pour the lime juice on top. Taste and adjust spices as desired. Serve with chips.

22 – Native American Succotash

This meal is nutritious and healthy, and the ingredients are not expensive at all. It's a Native American recipe that many city-dwelling Americans adopted during the Great Depression.

Makes 6-8 Servings

Cooking + Prep Time: 1 hour & 15 minutes + 3-4 hours soaking time

Ingredients:

- 2 pounds of beans, lima
- Salt, kosher, as desired
- Pepper, ground, as desired
- 3 quarts of water, filtered
- 3 cups of corn on cob, sliced off cob
- 3 or 4 onions, pearl or wild
- 2 tbsp. of bacon fat, melted
- 2 pieces ham, smoked

Instructions:

1. Soak the lima beans for 3-4 hours so they can soften, then drain well.

2. Add water in pot and bring to boil. Add beans and cook for 10-12 minutes. Add onions and corn. Season as desired.

3. Cook on low heat for an hour. Serve.

23 – Butternut Squash & Bell Pepper Soup

This is a wonderful soup for cold days or when you want something filling. If served for lunch, it will easily hold you over until dinnertime.

Makes 2-4 Servings

Cooking + Prep Time: 55 minutes

Ingredients:

- 1 butternut squash, peeled, cubed
- 1 large onion, yellow
- 1 bell pepper, red
- 4 cups of broth, vegetable or turkey
- Pepper, black, as desired
- Garlic, as desired
- Salt, kosher, as desired

Instructions:

1. Peel, then cut squash into cubes. Remove core and seeds. Chop onion.

2. Place ingredients in pan or skillet. Cook till squash has become tender.

3. Place heated ingredients into a food processor. Mix with the broth. Blend till it reaches the consistency you desire.

4. Place red bell pepper in pan. Sauté and allow to cook till tender.

5. Pour food processor mixture into bowl. Top with red peppers. Serve.

24 – Native Frybread

This is an underestimated recipe from Native American heritage. It's easy to make and truly a delight to enjoy and share.

Makes Various # of Servings

Cooking + Prep Time: 35 minutes

Ingredients:

- 1 cup of flour, all-purpose
- 1/2 tsp. of salt, kosher
- 3/4 cup of milk, whole
- 2 tsp. of baking soda, pure

To fry: oil, vegetable

Instructions:

1. Mix all ingredients together in large bowl. Knead till it forms a uniform dough.

2. Make small square or round batches of dough.

3. Fry them in large pan till both sides are golden brown in color. Serve.

25 – Vegetable Sauté

This is an easy, quick way to prepare vegetables. You can use the listed veggies or others you prefer, and it will always turn out delicious.

Makes 4-6 Servings

Cooking + Prep Time: 25 minutes

Ingredients:

- 2 tbsp. of oil, vegetable
- 2 or 3 chopped squash, yellow
- 2 or 3 chopped zucchini
- 2 cups of bell peppers, red, yellow and orange
- 1 to 2 cups of mushrooms, sliced
- 3 large tomatoes, sliced
- 1 cup of florets of broccoli
- 1 cup of cauliflower

Instructions:

1. Heat 2 tbsp. of oil in skillet on med. heat.

2. Cover pan with a single layer of veggies. Sprinkle with your favorite condiment. Cook on med. heat for two minutes, then turn.

3. Reduce heat to low. Cover skillet. Simmer till veggies have become tender and serve.

26 – Gitigan Salad

This salad uses delicious cherry tomatoes. You can use tomatoes from your own garden or purchase them at your local farmer's market. Either way, it's a tasty dish!

Makes 8 Servings

Cooking + Prep Time: 1 & 3/4 hours + 8 hours soaking time for beans

Ingredients:

For salad

- 2 bunches of kale, fresh
- 4 sprigs of thyme, fresh
- 1 & 1/2 cups of whole rice, wild
- 3 cups of broth, vegetable
- 1 cup of cooked beans, black
- 1 cup of rinsed, halved tomatoes, cherry
- 1/2 cup of cheese, Parmesan or Romano, grated

For dressing

- 1 fresh lemon
- 1 tbsp. of lemon zest, grated
- 1/4 cup of oil, olive
- 1/4 tsp. of salt, kosher
- Pepper, fresh-ground

Instructions:

1. Soak the beans for eight hours or overnight. Drain well.

2. Add the beans to large pot of filtered water. Boil till done, one to two hours. Set aside and allow to cool.

3. As beans cook, use that time to cook the rice. Rinse it well in medium bowl of cold, filtered water, then drain.

4. Add the broth, thyme and rice to pot. Simmer for 20-25 minutes. Remove pot from the heat. Cover the pot. Allow rice to set for five minutes or so. Remove thyme and discard. Use a fork to fluff the rice. Set it aside so it can cool.

5. Wash kale. Remove ribs. Slice thinly in ribbons. Squeeze gently to rid kale of excess water.

6. In large bowl, add kale, a bit of salt and a drizzling of oil. Massage kale till it begins to wilt and soften, two to three minutes. Set kale aside.

7. To prepare the dressing, whisk lemon juice & zest with kosher salt and ground pepper, along with 1/4 cup oil in medium bowl.

8. Add rice, beans and tomatoes to kale in large bowl. Sprinkle the cheese on top. Drizzle with dressing. Combine by tossing and serve.

27 – Dakota Wojapi Berry Sauce

This sauce serves so many purposes. It can be dolloped on pancakes or cheesecake or paired with savory grilled meats.

Makes 4-6 Servings

Cooking + Prep Time: 25 minutes

Ingredients:

- 4 cups of frozen/thawed or fresh blueberries
- 1 to 2 tbsp. corn starch
- Maple syrup, pure
- 1/4 cup of water, filtered

Instructions:

1. Simmer water and berries in pan on low heat, occasionally stirring.

2. Once berries have broken down and created sauce, spoon out some. Whisk in the corn starch. Whisk till the corn starch is dissolved completely. Add back to remainder of sauce.

3. Sweeten till the taste is as you prefer, using maple syrup.

4. Serve over ice cream, corn bread, pancakes, etc.

28 – Wild Rice Burgers

The wild rice in this recipe helps to keep your burgers delicious and moist. The texture and flavor give hamburgers a unique and subtle character all their own.

Makes 4 Servings

Cooking + Prep Time: 35 minutes

Ingredients:

- 1 lb. of beef, ground
- 2 cups of wild rice, cooked

Optional: 2 minced cloves of garlic

Optional: 1 tbsp. of thyme, dried or fresh

- Salt, kosher and pepper, ground, as desired

Instructions:

1. Mix ground beef, wild rice and optional ingredients (if using) well in large mixing bowl. Combine till you have a consistent texture.

2. Prepare grill for med-high heat.

3. Form the mixture in patties. Cook on an outdoor grill on both sides till done as you desire. Serve like you would any hamburger.

29 – Peach & Blueberry Salsa

Blueberries have been a significant source of food for Native Americans in the Great Lakes area for many years, and they still are today. This salsa includes vegetables, too, and is wonderful for dipping tortilla chips.

Makes Various # of Servings

Cooking + Prep Time: 10 minutes

Ingredients:

- 1 cup of blueberries, fresh
- 1 cup of peaches, diced
- 1 to 2 cups of tomatoes, diced
- 2 green onions, minced
- 1 lime, fresh
- Salt, kosher, as desired
- Pepper, ground, as desired

Optional: 1 or 2 minced garlic cloves

Optional: 1 tbsp. of cilantro, minced

Instructions:

1. Mix ingredients well in large-sized bowl.

2. Serve with chips or other dipping ingredients.

30 – Cherokee Fried Hominy

The Cherokee lived in North America starting as far back as 1000 A.D. They used hominy because it was easy to make for the limited cooking techniques of the time. They still use it today.

Makes 4 Servings

Cooking + Prep Time: 45 minutes

Ingredients:

- 2 bacon strips
- 2 cups of hominy
- 1 green onion, medium
- Salt, kosher & pepper, ground, as desired

Instructions:

1. Drain the hominy from can through sieve into bowl. Set aside for now.

2. Heat oven-proof skillet over med-high.

3. Add the bacon. Fry till crisp on both sides. Remove the bacon from skillet and set it aside.

4. Chop green onions in small-sized pieces.

5. Add the onions to skillet. Fry over high heat.

6. Crumble the bacon and add into skillet.

7. When onions begin frying, add the hominy. Add pepper as desired.

8. Cook for 5-10 minutes on high heat. Reduce heat to low and cook 5 more minutes. Serve.

There are many desserts that were first made by Native Americans. Here are some of the best...

31 – Corn Meal Cookies

This Native American recipe is originally quite old, but it has been somewhat modernized as the years have passed. It's a slightly different-tasting cookie, but delicious.

Makes 18-24 Cookies

Cooking + Prep Time: 35 minutes

Ingredients:

- 1/3 tsp. of salt, kosher
- 3/4 cup of sugar, granulated (you can use less if you prefer)
- 3/4 cup of margarine, softened
- 1/2 cup of molasses, syrup or honey
- 2 tsp. of vanilla extract, pure
- 2 beaten eggs, large
- 1/2 cup of cornmeal
- 1 & 3/4 cup of flour, all-purpose
- 2 tsp. of baking powder, pure

Optional ingredients

- 3/4 cup of nuts, dried berries, raisins or chocolate chips

Instructions:

1. Preheat the oven to 350F.

2. Cream together the margarine, salt and sugar. Add the egg and vanilla. Add honey, molasses or syrup. Beat till creamy and blended well.

3. In a separate, medium bowl, mix flour, baking powder and cornmeal together well. Add this mixture gradually to creamy mixture from step 2.

4. Add whatever optional ingredients you desire.

5. Pat dough in small-sized patties using your hands. Place on a greased cookie sheet.

6. Bake in 350F oven for 12-15 minutes, till they are light and golden brown.

7. Remove from the cookie sheet. Allow to cool. Serve.

32 – Grilled Pineapple

It's easy to grill pineapple, and it's such a sweet treat. You can serve it as a simple dessert or add it to steak or other types of meat to freshen the taste.

Makes 2-3 Servings

Cooking + Prep Time: 45 minutes + 4 – 24 hours fruit soaking time

Ingredients:

- 1 pineapple, large
- 1 cup of maple syrup, pure
- 1/2 tbsp. of cinnamon, ground

Instructions:

1. Cut top and bottom off pineapple.

2. Cut fruit lengthwise down center. Quarter.

3. Slice tough mid-section off quarters.

4. Remove tough skin. You can use a potato peeler end for digging out embedded eyes.

5. Cut in long slices. Marinate slices in large plastic bag with maple syrup.

6. Soak pineapple for four hours minimum, 24 hours maximum.

7. Place fruit on a heated grill. Cook for a couple of minutes per side. Serve.

33 – Cherokee Grape Dumplings

This dessert is loved by many people in the Cherokee and Choctaw Nations. Wild grapes are difficult to find today, so you can use Concord grapes and prepare grape juice instead. It still tastes wonderful.

Makes 8 Servings

Cooking + Prep Time: 35 minutes

Ingredients:

- 8 cups of grape juice, unsweetened
- 2 cups of sugar, granulated
- 1 cup of grapes, seedless

For dumplings

- 2 tbsp. of melted shortening
- 1 tsp. of baking powder, pure
- 1 cup of water, filtered
- 3 cups of flour, all-purpose
- 1 tsp. of salt, kosher

Instructions:

1. Bring the grape juice to high boil, along with sugar. Add the grapes.

2. To make dumplings, combine flour, sugar, baking powder & kosher salt in medium bowl. Mix thoroughly.

3. Cut shortening into flour mixture. It should look like coarse meal. Stir water into dough. With your hands, form dough into one ball.

4. Flour work surface lightly. Pat dough ball into a round disc.

5. Sprinkle dough with thin flour coat. Roll dough out till its thickness is roughly 1/4".

6. Using all dough, cut into 2" squares. There will usually be 16 squares or more.

7. Bring grape juice to boil in large pot.

8. Drop the dough squares in juice.

9. Cook on high heat for five minutes or so per batch.

10. Cover the pot. Simmer for 10-12 minutes. Serve plain or with cream.

34 – Dessert Fruit Salad

Fruit salad is a perfect dish for any season. It is tasty, sweet and filled with vitamins. It will stay fresh in the refrigerator for a couple of days if you have leftovers.

Makes 2-3 Servings

Cooking + Prep Time: 15 minutes

Ingredients:

- 1 chopped apple
- 1 peeled, seeded, sectioned orange
- 1 peeled, then de-seeded, cubed mango, ripe – not squishy
- 1 thinly sliced banana

Instructions:

1. Chop the fruits into slices or cubes, as desired. Place in large-sized serving bowl and serve.

2. Tightly cover any leftovers. They will stay fresh for two days.

35 – Choctaw Autumn Cake

Native Americans introduced the first settlers to winter squash and pumpkin, sharing their cooking methods, too. This recipe uses pumpkin in a unique and flavorful cake.

Makes 12-16 slices

Cooking + Prep Time: 1 hour & 25 minutes

Ingredients:

- 2 cups of flour, all-purpose
- 2 cups of sugar, granulated
- 1 tsp. of salt, kosher
- 2 tsp. of cinnamon, ground
- 2 tsp. of baking soda, pure
- 1 tbsp. of cocoa, unsweetened
- 1 & 1/2 cups of pumpkin, canned or flesh from pumpkin
- 1 & 1/2 cups of oil, vegetable or corn
- 4 beaten eggs, large
- 1 tsp. of vanilla, pure

To top: whipped cream, as desired

Instructions:

1. Preheat the oven to 350F.

2. Oil, then flour Bundt cake pan generously.

3. In large bowl, combine the flour, baking soda, sugar, cocoa and cinnamon.

4. Add the pumpkin, eggs, oil and vanilla. Blend thoroughly.

5. Pour batter into Bundt pan prepared above.

6. Bake cake in 350F oven for 40 to 50 minutes.

7. Turn cake out on wire rack for cooling. Serve while warm or after cake has cooled, top with whipped cream, if you like.

Conclusion

This Native American cookbook has shown you…

How to use different ingredients to affect unique, tribal tastes in many types of dishes.

How can you include Native American recipes in your home repertoire?

You can…

- Make Native American Succotash and Gitigan Salad, which you may not have heard of them before. They are just as tasty as they sound.
- Cook soups and stews, which are widely served in homes of Native Americans. Find ingredients in meat & produce or frozen food sections of your local grocery store.
- Enjoy making the delectable seafood dishes of Native Americans, including salmon and catfish. Fish is a mainstay, and there are SO many ways to make it great.
- Make dishes using cornmeal and fresh produce in cold-weather recipes. There is something about them that **Makes** them more authentic.
- Make all kinds of desserts like dessert fruit salad and Choctaw Autumn cake, which will surely tempt anyone with a sweet tooth.

Enjoy these recipes with your family and friends!

About the Author

Allie Allen developed her passion for the culinary arts at the tender age of five when she would help her mother cook for their large family of 8. Even back then, her family knew this would be more than a hobby for the young Allie and when she graduated from high school, she applied to cooking school in London. It had always been a dream of the young chef to study with some of Europe's best and she made it happen by attending the Chef Academy of London.

After graduation, Allie decided to bring her skills back to North America and open up her own restaurant. After 10 successful years as head chef and owner, she decided to sell her business and pursue other career avenues. This monumental decision led Allie to her true calling, teaching. She also started to write e-books for her students to study at home for practice. She is now the proud author of several e-books and gives private and semi-private cooking lessons to a range of students at all levels of experience.

Stay tuned for more from this dynamic chef and teacher when she releases more informative e-books on cooking and baking in the near future. Her work is infused with stores and anecdotes you will love!

Author's Afterthoughts

I can't tell you how grateful I am that you decided to read my book. My most heartfelt thanks that you took time out of your life to choose my work and I hope you find benefit within these pages.

There are so many books available today that offer similar content so that makes it even more humbling that you decided to buying mine.

Tell me what you thought! I am eager to hear your opinion and ideas on what you read as are others who are looking for a good book to buy. Leave a review on Amazon.com so others can benefit from your wisdom!

With much thanks,

Allie Allen

Printed in Great Britain
by Amazon